THE
TOTALLY
CHOCOLATE
COOKBOOK

THE
TOTALLY
CHOCOLATE
COOKBOOK

*By Helene Siegel
and
Karen Gillingham*

CELESTIAL ARTS
BERKELEY, CALIFORNIA

The Totally Chocolate Cookbook is produced by
becker&mayer!, Ltd.

Printed in Singapore.

Cover design and illustration: Bob Greisen
Interior design and typesetting: Susan Hernday
Interior illustrations: Carolyn Vibbert

Library of Congress Cataloging-in-Publication Data:
Siegel, Helene.
Totally Chocolate / by Helene Siegel and Karen Gillingham
    p.   cm.
    ISBN 0-89087-805-6
    1. Cookery (Chocolate) 2. Chocolate   I. Title
    TX767.C5S55 1996
    641.6'374—dc20   96-14031
                               CIP

Celestial Arts Publishing
P.O. Box 7123
Berkeley, CA 94707

Other cookbooks in this series:
The Totally Burgers Cookbook
The Totally Camping Cookbook
The Totally Pancakes & Waffles Cookbook

FOR FUZZY—
FOR BEING THERE,
AND EATING CHOCOLATE.

CONTENTS

INTRODUCTION

Anyone who spends any time in the kitchen eventually comes to realize that what he or she is looking for is the perfect chocolate cake.

> —Laurie Colwin, author of Home Cooking: A Writer in the Kitchen

As cookbook authors, it is an honor and a privilege to work with chocolate— the most sensuous ingredient in the cupboard. On the other hand, the responsibility is daunting.

It's a challenge to cover the intricacies of tempering chocolate or forming a perfect chocolate leaf, while including all the basics a good home cook should not be without. a glossy and a fluffy frosting, a delectable pudding, the best brownies, a chocolate layer cake for children's birthday parties, the richest hot cocoa, cupcakes to swoon for, and a few wonderful cookies to keep the little monsters happy.

We decided to forgo the truly baroque and the highly technical. For those creations and complete lessons in the essential mystery that is chocolate, there are other, longer cookbooks by master crafts-people such as Alice Medrich and Rose Levy Beranbaum.

But if it is a quick and delicious chocolate fix you are looking for, you have come to the right book. Just follow the recipes carefully—chocolate does not like to be fooled with—and many happy chocolate moments are guaranteed to follow.

BEST BREADS

CHOCOLATE
SOUR CHERRY MUFFINS

These are delicious enough to pass as cupcakes.

$3/4$ cup dried sour cherries or cranberries
$1/4$ cup Kirsch
1 stick butter
6 ounces semisweet chocolate, chopped
3 eggs
$1/2$ cup sugar
$2/3$ cup sour cream
$3/4$ cup all-purpose flour
2 teaspoons baking powder
$1/2$ teaspoon baking soda

Preheat oven to 375 degrees F. Grease muffin tins or line with paper cups.

Combine dried cherries or cranberries with Kirsch in small saucepan. Set over low heat until liquid is absorbed. Set aside to cool.

In heavy medium saucepan, combine butter and chocolate. Cook over low heat, stirring constantly, until melted and smooth. Cool.

In a mixing bowl, cream together eggs and sugar until light and fluffy. Beat in sour cream. Pour in chocolate mixture and stir to combine.

In another bowl, stir together flour, baking powder, and soda. Add to the chocolate mixture and mix just until flour disappears. Gently stir in cherries or cranberries and fill muffin cups to the top. Bake 20 to 25 minutes, until a tester comes out clean.

MAKES 12

Semisweet and bittersweet chocolate may be used interchangeably. According to FDA regulations, bittersweet must contain at least 35 percent cocoa liquor and semisweet at least 15 percent. Both are terrific for baking and dessert making.

ORANGE CHOCOLATE
TEA BREAD

The combination of tart oranges and bittersweet chocolate is irresistible.

1 stick butter, softened
$3/4$ cup sugar
2 eggs
1 tablespoon plus 1 teaspoon grated
    orange zest
2 tablespoons orange liqueur such as
    Grand Marnier
$3/4$ cup half-and-half
2 cups all-purpose flour
1 tablespoon baking powder
$1/4$ teaspoon salt
$1/2$ cup chopped walnuts
7 ounces semisweet chocolate, chopped
1 tablespoon water

Preheat oven to 350 degrees F. Grease or spray a 9 x 5 x 3-inch loaf pan.

Cream together the butter and sugar until light and fluffy. Add the eggs and beat well. Beat in orange zest and a tablespoon of liqueur. Pour in half-and-half and beat to combine. (Do not be concerned with curdling.)

In another bowl, stir and toss together flour, baking powder, and salt. Add to butter mixture and gently beat just to combine. Stir in nuts and 4 ounces chopped chocolate. Spoon batter into prepared pan and smooth top. Bake 1 hour, until top is golden. Cool in pan on rack. Invert onto serving platter and cool completely.

When bread is cool, combine remaining chocolate with water and remaining tablespoon of orange liqueur in heavy saucepan. Place over low heat and melt, stirring constantly. Spread evenly over top and chill to set.

MAKES 1 LOAF

GERMAN CHOCOLATE MUFFINS

1 stick butter
6 ounces sweet German chocolate
1³/₄ cups all-purpose flour
2 teaspoons baking powder
¹/₂ teaspoon baking soda
3 eggs
¹/₃ cup sugar
²/₃ cup buttermilk
Coconut Pecan Filling

Preheat oven to 375 degrees F. Grease muffin tins or line with paper cups.

In small saucepan, combine butter and chocolate. Cook over low heat, stirring frequently, until melted and smooth. Set aside to cool.

Stir and toss together flour, baking powder, and soda.

In medium bowl, whisk eggs with sugar until light. Stir in buttermilk. Stir in chocolate mixture. Add dry ingredients and stir just until flour disappears. Fill prepared muffin cups. Bake 20 to 25 minutes or until tester comes out clean.

Cool in pan 5 minutes, then turn out onto rack and cool completely. Split each muffin in half horizontally. Fill with Coconut Pecan Filling.

COCONUT PECAN FILLING
3/4 cup confectioners' sugar
1 stick butter, softened
1 teaspoon vanilla
3/4 cup flaked coconut, lightly toasted
3/4 cup chopped pecans
2 ounces sweet chocolate, grated

Cream together sugar and butter. Stir in vanilla, coconut, pecans, and chocolate.

MAKES 12

CHOCOLATE WALNUT TEA BREAD

Cut in thin slices and serve with softened cream cheese or creme fraiche for afternoon tea.

1³/₄ cups all-purpose flour
1 tablespoon baking powder
1 teaspoon baking soda
1 stick butter, softened
1 cup sugar
2 eggs
2 teaspoons vanilla
¹/₂ cup Dutch cocoa
1 cup buttermilk
³/₄ cup walnuts, chopped

Preheat oven to 350 degrees F. Lightly grease a 9 x 5 x 3-inch loaf pan.

Combine flour, baking powder, and soda in bowl. Mix with fork.

In the bowl of an electric mixer, cream together butter and sugar. Add eggs and vanilla and lightly beat until smooth. Sprinkle in cocoa and beat until smooth. Pour in buttermilk and mix.

Add flour mixture and beat just until flour disappears. Stir in nuts. Spoon batter into prepared pan, smooth the top, and bake about 1 hour, until tester comes out clean. Cool in pan or rack. Invert to remove and thoroughly cool.

MAKES 1 LOAF

Unsweetened cocoa is the powder that results when cocoa butter or fat has been removed from cocoa beans. Dutch processed cocoa has been alkalized to neutralize its natural acidity. We prefer Dutch cocoa for baking for its darker color and mellower flavor.

CHOCOLATE-ALMOND CINNAMON ROLLS

$^1/_3$ cup milk
$^1/_2$ stick butter, cut in pieces
3 tablespoons sugar
$^1/_2$ teaspoon salt
1 ($^1/_4$-ounce) package dry yeast
$^1/_4$ cup warm water
$3^1/_2$ cups all-purpose flour
2 eggs, room temperature
Chocolate Cinnamon Filling (follows)
$^1/_4$ cup semisweet chocolate chips, melted

In small saucepan, combine milk, butter, sugar, and salt. Cook over medium-low heat, stirring until mixture reaches about 110 degrees F.

In large bowl, sprinkle yeast over warm water. Pour in milk mixture and blend. Stir in $1^1/_2$ cups flour, blending well. Beat in eggs, then 1 cup more flour. Turn dough out onto

floured surface and knead until
smooth, about 10 minutes, adding
more flour as needed to prevent sticking.
Place dough in oiled bowl, turn, cover, and let
rise in warm place about 1½ hours or until doubled.

Grease 12 x 9-inch baking pan.

Punch dough down and knead on floured surface about 1 minute. Roll out to 18 x 12-inch rec-
tangle. Sprinkle Chocolate Cinnamon Filling
over dough to within ¾ inch of edges. Starting
from long side, roll dough, pinching to seal
seams. Cut dough into 12 slices across width and
arrange, cut-side up, in pan. Cover and let rise in
warm place about 45 minutes or until doubled.

Preheat oven to 350 degrees F.

Bake about 25 minutes or until golden. Cool
10 minutes, then drizzle with melted chocolate.

MAKES 12

CHOCOLATE CINNAMON FILLING

$3/4$ cup semisweet chocolate chips
$1/2$ cup finely chopped almonds
$1/4$ cup brown sugar
2 teaspoons cinnamon
$1/2$ stick butter, melted and cooled

In small bowl, combine chocolate chips, almonds, brown sugar, and cinnamon. Add butter and toss with fork to combine.

MAKES 12

Chocolate chips are made of semisweet chocolate, specially treated to hold its shape when heated.

MEANINGFUL CAKES, PIES & TARTS

DEVIL'S FOOD CUPCAKES

These should be every child's birthright—deep, dark chocolate cupcakes for bringing to school and sharing.

> 4 ounces unsweetened chocolate, chopped
> 1¾ cups all-purpose flour
> 1 teaspoon salt
> 1 teaspoon baking soda
> 1 stick butter, softened
> 1 cup brown sugar
> ¾ cup sugar
> 3 eggs
> 1 teaspoon vanilla extract
> 1 cup milk
> "No-Fail Fudge Frosting" or "Sour Cream Chocolate Frosting" (see pages 76 and 79) and sprinkles

Preheat oven to 350 degrees F. Coat 18 muffin cups with butter or line with paper cups.

Melt chocolate in the microwave
or in the top of a double boiler. Cool.

Combine flour, salt, and baking soda in
a bowl.

In another bowl, cream together butter and
sugars until smooth and fluffy. Add eggs, one
at a time, beating well between additions. Beat
in vanilla.

Add flour mixture and milk in three parts,
alternating liquid and dry, and beating and
scraping down bowl between additions. Spoon
into prepared tins and bake 25 to 30 minutes,
until a tester comes out clean. Cool slightly,
turn out, and cool completely on rack before
frosting.

MAKES 18

---

*German chocolate is a sweet version of semisweet
chocolate.*

QUICK CRAZY CAKE

Here is an easy, unfussy layer cake for children's parties. It has just the right amount of richness for younger palates.

1 stick butter, softened
2 eggs
1½ cups brown sugar
2 ounces unsweetened chocolate, melted and cooled
2 cups all-purpose flour
1 teaspoon baking soda
½ teaspoon salt
¾ cup milk
¼ cup vinegar
1 teaspoon vanilla
raspberry jam
"Sour Cream Chocolate Frosting" (see page 79)

Preheat oven to 350 degrees F. Line two 8-inch round cake pans with parchment.

In bowl of an electric mixer, combine butter, eggs, brown sugar, and chocolate. Beat about 3 minutes at high speed.

In another bowl, combine flour, baking soda, and salt. Stir and toss with fork.

Combine milk, vinegar, and vanilla in glass measuring cup. Add flour mixture and milk mixture to chocolate in 2 batches, alternating dry and liquid ingredients. Beat and scrape down the bowl between additions. Beat an additional minute at medium-low speed.

Pour batter into prepared pans, smoothing tops. Bake until sides pull away and tester comes out clean, 35 to 40 minutes. Cool in pans on rack. Invert and peel paper. Place bottom layer on cake plate and spread with an even layer of raspberry jam. Top with second layer and frost top and sides.

SERVES 12

MEXICAN CHOCOLATE CAKE

The combination of cinnamon and almonds with chocolate goes back to the Aztecs.

1/4 cup vegetable shortening
2 cups sugar
2 eggs, separated
4 ounces unsweetened chocolate, melted and cooled
2 cups cake flour
2 teaspoons baking powder
2 teaspoons ground cinnamon
1 teaspoon salt
1 1/2 cups milk
1 teaspoon almond extract
1 cup finely chopped almonds, toasted
"More Than Chocolate Ganache" (see page 74)
ground cinnamon and chopped toasted almonds for garnish

Preheat oven to 350 degrees F. Grease
and flour two 9-inch round cake pans.

In large bowl, cream shortening with 1
cup sugar and egg yolks. Add chocolate and
blend thoroughly.

Sift together flour, baking powder, cinnamon,
and salt. Add dry ingredients and milk to chocolate mixture in batches, alternating and blending
well between additions. Stir in almond extract
and finely chopped almonds.

In separate bowl, beat egg whites until frothy.
Gradually beat in remaining sugar, beating until
stiff. Fold into batter. Pour into prepared pans
and bake 30 to 40 minutes, or until cake springs
back when lightly pressed in center. Cool in pans
on rack. Invert to remove and cool completely.
Fill and frost with ganache. Lightly sprinkle top
with cinnamon and chopped toasted almonds.

SERVES 8

CHOCOLATE ALMOND TORTE

Combining chocolates gives this elegant flourless cake extra complexity and flavor. This is a good choice for Passover.

8 ounces semisweet chocolate, chopped
2 ounces unsweetened chocolate, chopped
6 egg yolks
8 egg whites
1¼ cup sugar
¾ cup finely ground almonds
1 tablespoon rum or vanilla
1 teaspoon almond extract
confectioners' sugar for dusting or whipped cream

Preheat oven to 350 degrees F. Coat a 9-inch springform pan with butter and line with parchment.

Melt the chocolates together in a bowl over simmering water or in the microwave. Cool.

In the bowl of an electric mixer, beat together the egg yolks, sugar, and almonds. Beat in rum or vanilla and almond extract. Pour in melted chocolate and beat well to combine.

In another bowl, whisk the egg whites until stiff peaks form. Gently stir whites into chocolate mixture—this is a thick, lumpy batter—and pour into pan. Bake about 50 minutes, until cake is set but moist—the tester should come out clean. Cool in pan on rack. Remove sides and sprinkle with confectioners' sugar or serve with dollop of whipped cream.

SERVES 10

CHOCOLATE TEA CAKE

Ever since we learned about this cake from Los Angeles chef Michael Roberts, it has served as our standby, quick-fix chocolate dessert. You can dress it up with a top coating of ganache (see page 74) or simply dust with confectioners' sugar—either way it is perfect.

6 ounces semisweet chocolate, chopped
1 stick butter, softened
$^2/_3$ cup sugar
3 eggs
$^1/_2$ cup cake flour
confectioners' sugar for dusting

Preheat oven to 350 degrees F. Line a 9-inch round cake pan with parchment.

Melt the chocolate in the top of a double boiler or in the microwave. Cool.

Beat the butter until light and fluffy. Beat in sugar. Pour in chocolate and mix to combine. Add the eggs, one at a time, beating well after each addition. Gently mix in the flour until it just disappears.

Pour into prepared pan, smooth the top, and bake about 25 minutes, until a tester comes out clean. Cool in pan on rack. Invert onto serving platter, peel paper, and dust top with confectioners' sugar.

SERVES 8

Milk chocolate is light in color and sweet in flavor because it contains milk solids, fats, and plenty of sugar. It was invented by Henri Nestlé, in Switzerland, after the invention of condensed milk. Many connoisseurs (and kids) swear by it for the taste and the way it melts in the mouth.

WHITE CHOCOLATE
PINEAPPLE TART

*The tartness of pineapple is the perfect foil for
white chocolate's sweetness.*

1 frozen pie crust
$^1/_2$ pineapple, halved lengthwise
3 tablespoons sugar
2 tablespoons rum
8 ounces white chocolate, chopped
1 cup heavy cream, cold
juice of 1 lime
7 egg whites

Prebake pie crust according to directions. Set
aside to cool.

Peel the pineapple and cut into thin slices
across width. Place in a bowl with 1 tablespoon of sugar and the rum. Toss well and
refrigerate.

Melt the chocolate in the top of a double boiler or in the microwave. Let cool.

Whip the cream until soft peaks form. Add 1 tablespoon of the sugar and the lime juice and continue beating until stiff peaks form. Gently fold in the chocolate.

In another bowl, whisk the egg whites until soft peaks form. Add the remaining tablespoon of sugar and continue beating until stiff peaks form. Fold the egg whites into the chocolate mixture.

Spoon the mousse into cooled pie shell, smoothing the top. Cover and chill about 4 hours. Arrange pineapple slices over top and chill an additional hour or more.

SERVES 8

Chocolate and the King are my only passions.
  —*Queen Maria Thérèse of France*

MUD PIE

For those who feel restraint has no place at the dessert table—a messy, gooey pile of chocolate and ice cream to play in.

1½ cups chocolate wafer crumbs
⅓ cup melted butter
2 ounces semisweet chocolate, chopped
1 tablespoon butter
2 teaspoons corn syrup
½ gallon coffee ice cream, softened
"Renee's Hot Fudge Sauce" (see page 80), whipped cream, and sliced, toasted almonds for garnish

Preheat oven to 350 degrees F.

Combine wafer crumbs and melted butter in medium bowl. Press over bottom and sides of 9-inch pie pan. Bake 8 minutes. Cool on rack.

In small saucepan, combine chocolate, butter, and corn syrup. Set over very low heat and stir until smooth. Using back of spoon, spread over bottom and partially up sides of cooled pie shell. Chill.

Pack ice cream into chilled crust, smoothing top. Freeze until firm. Serve topped with "Renee's Hot Fudge Sauce," whipped cream, and almonds.

SERVES 8

It appears to me that when a magazine wants to increase its circulation, they simply have to use a photograph of a mouth-watering, three-layer chocolate cake..

—*Maida Heatter, author of* Maida Heatter's Book of Great Chocolate Desserts

MARBLEIZED MINI-TARTS

1 stick butter, softened
1/2 cup sugar
3/4 teaspoon vanilla
1/2 cup Dutch cocoa
1 cup all-purpose flour
4 ounces white chocolate, chopped
5 ounces semisweet chocolate, chopped
3/4 cup heavy cream
1/4 cup Frangelico

With electric mixer, beat butter, sugar, and vanilla until creamy. Beat in cocoa. Add flour, and using fork or fingers, work into stiff dough. Divide evenly into 12 portions. Press onto bottom and sides of twelve 3-inch tartlet pans. Pierce bottoms all over with fork. Chill.

Preheat oven to 375 degrees F.

Arrange chilled pans on baking sheet and bake 8 minutes. Pierce with fork again and bake 4 minutes longer. Cool on rack

Place white chocolate in small bowl and semisweet in another. In small saucepan, bring cream to simmer, stir in Frangelico, and return to simmer. Pour $1/2$ cup hot cream mixture into each bowl of chocolate and stir until smooth.

Carefully remove crusts from pans. Fill each two-thirds full with dark chocolate filling. Spoon 3 small distinct pools of white filling onto dark filling. Draw tip of knife through fillings to marbleize. Chill to set.

MAKES 12

Unsweetened chocolate, used for baking and dessert making, gives a darker, richer color to the finished product. It contains no sugar and is rich in cocoa butter. Each ounce of unsweetened chocolate in a recipe calls for about half a cup of sugar to balance the flavor.

VANILLA FUDGE
CHEESECAKE

1½ cups chocolate wafer crumbs
½ stick butter, melted
¾ cup plus 2 tablespoons sugar
1½ pounds cream cheese, softened
3 eggs
1 cup sour cream
1½ teaspoons vanilla
4 ounces semisweet chocolate, melted

Preheat oven to 350 degrees F.

In small bowl, combine chocolate crumbs, butter, and 2 tablespoons sugar. Press into bottom and partially up sides of 9-inch springform pan. Freeze 5 minutes, then bake 10 minutes. Set aside.

Reduce heat to 300 degrees F.

In large bowl of electric mixer, beat cream cheese, remaining sugar, eggs, sour cream, and vanilla until smooth. Transfer $3^1/_2$ cups mixture to another bowl and blend in melted chocolate. Pour white mixture into chocolate crust. Spoon on chocolate mixture in 5 or 6 distinct pools. Draw knife tip through mixture to marbleize. Bake $1^1/_4$ hours. Turn oven off and let set in oven $1^1/_2$ hours. Chill before serving.

SERVES 16

The Problem with Chocolate
The only bad chocolate is ruined chocolate. If liquid is added to melted chocolate too soon, or a drop gets in while it is melting, it will harden into a grainy mass. This is called seizing. To save chocolate after it has seized, quickly beat in a tablespoon of vegetable shortening at a time, until it is restored to a smooth consistency

CHOCOLATE
PECAN PIE

1/4 cup brown sugar
1/4 cup sugar
3/4 cup light corn syrup
2 tablespoons Dutch cocoa
2 eggs plus 2 egg yolks
2 tablespoons butter, melted
1 1/2 cups coarsely chopped pecans
1 unbaked 9-inch pie crust
1 ounce semisweet chocolate, melted

Preheat oven to 425 degrees F.

In large bowl, using wire whisk, beat sugars, corn syrup, cocoa, egg, and egg yolks until light. Stir in butter, then add pecans. Pour into crust and bake 10 minutes. Reduce heat to 350 degrees F and bake another 25 minutes, until firm. Cool on rack. Drizzle melted chocolate over top of cooled pie.

SERVES 8 TO 10

HOMEMADE
CANDIES
&
COCOAS

CHOCOLATE
PEANUT BUTTER BALLS

1 (16-ounce) jar creamy peanut butter
1 pound confectioners' sugar
2 sticks butter, softened
12 ounces semisweet chocolate chips

In large bowl, combine peanut butter, sugar, and butter. Beat until well blended and smooth. Break off pieces and roll into 1-inch balls. Arrange on baking sheet and refrigerate 30 minutes.

Line another baking sheet with waxed paper.

Place chocolate chips in top of double boiler. Melt over simmering water, stirring occasionally, until melted and smooth.

Using wood pick or skewer, dip balls into chocolate to coat completely, letting excess drip back into pan. Set balls on prepared baking sheet. Store in refrigerator.

MAKES ABOUT 3½ POUNDS CANDY

Melting Chocolate

To melt chocolate, use either the top of a double boiler or a microwave. A double boiler can be improvised by bringing an inch or two of water to a boil in a small pot. Select a mixing bowl that nests in the pot without touching the water. Place chopped chocolate in the bowl, reduce heat to low, and stir until melted and smooth. Remove immediately.

In the microwave, place chopped chocolate in a container or bowl and cook at high power for 1 minute. Remove and stir. If solids still remain, return to high power and cook in 10 second intervals--removing, stirring, and checking since chocolate can burn quickly in the microwave.

Chocolate that is combined with butter and a liquid is not as difficult to work with and can be melted in a heavy pan directly over low heat. Just stir it frequently and watch it carefully.

TRUFFLE SQUARES

$1/2$ cup heavy cream
8 ounces semisweet chocolate, chopped
2 tablespoons butter
$1/3$ cup plus 3 tablespoons Dutch cocoa
$1/2$ teaspoon vanilla
pinch of salt
$1/3$ cup confectioners' sugar

Line 8 x 5-inch loaf pan with plastic wrap, letting plastic overhang the sides.

Bring cream to simmer in heavy saucepan over medium-high heat. Add chocolate and butter and cook over low heat, stirring, until melted and smooth. Remove from heat and stir in 3 tablespoons cocoa along with vanilla and salt. Pour into prepared pan, smoothing top. Cover and refrigerate until firm, about 2 hours.

Remove from pan by lifting plastic. Carefully peel plastic and cut into 1-inch squares. Transfer pieces to baking tray and chill.

Before serving, sift powdered sugar with remaining $\frac{1}{3}$ cup cocoa into bowl or plastic bag. Drop squares, 3 or 4 at a time, into mixture and toss or shake lightly to coat. Store in sealed container.

MAKES 32

For HAZELNUT TRUFFLES: Omit vanilla and stir in 2 teaspoons Frangelico. Toss chilled squares in finely chopped toasted hazelnuts to coat.

For COCONUT-ALMOND TRUFFLES: Substitute almond extract for vanilla. Toss chilled squares in sweetened flaked coconut.

NO-FUSS FUDGE
WITH TOASTED ALMONDS

$1^1/_3$ cups sugar
2 tablespoons butter
$^1/_4$ teaspoon salt
$^1/_2$ cup evaporated milk
2 cups semisweet chocolate chips
1 teaspoon vanilla
$^1/_4$ teaspoon almond extract
$^3/_4$ cup almonds, toasted and chopped

Line an 8-inch square baking pan with plastic wrap, letting wrap overhang sides.

Combine sugar, butter, salt, and milk in heavy saucepan. Cook over medium heat, stirring constantly, until mixture comes to a boil. Reduce heat and simmer 5 minutes, stirring constantly. Remove from heat and stir in chocolate chips until melted and smooth. Stir in vanilla, almond extract, and almonds and transfer to prepared pan. Chill until firm, about 3 hours. Remove from pan by lifting plastic. Carefully peel wrap and cut fudge into 1¼-inch squares. Store, covered, in refrigerator.

MAKES 36

Chocolate Storage
Wrap chocolate in foil and store in a cool, dark place, not the refrigerator. Temperature changes affect chocolate's appearance and usability. When cocoa butter separates and floats to the surface, a grayish film called fat bloom is formed. Though unsightly, it does not affect flavor or meltability. When sugar granules float to the surface, however, causing sugar bloom, texture and meltability have been compromised. Chocolate with sugar bloom should not be used for baking. Properly stored chocolate can keep a good long time, if nobody finds it.

HOT CHOCOLATE—
THE DRINK

Once you've tasted the French version of hot cocoa, instant mixes will never be the same.

2 ounces semisweet chocolate, chopped
1 cup milk

Place the chocolate in a small pan with 2 tablespoons of the milk. Cook over low heat, stirring frequently, until melted. Pour in the remaining milk, turn up the heat and bring nearly to a boil. Whisk well to disperse chocolate and pour into cups. (Serve with pitcher of warm milk to be added as desired.) Can be made at night and reheated in the morning.

SERVES 2

DEEPEST,
DARKEST
COOKIES

SHORTBREADS FROM HEAVEN

We have a weakness for shortbreads, and as for chocolate—has it been named a food group yet?

2 sticks butter, softened
1 cup confectioners' sugar
1 teaspoon vanilla
$1\frac{1}{2}$ cups cake flour
$\frac{1}{2}$ cup Dutch cocoa
$\frac{1}{4}$ teaspoon salt

Preheat oven to 350 degrees F.

Beat butter at low speed on electric mixer until smooth and fluffy. Add sugar and vanilla and beat until smooth.

In another bowl, combine flour, cocoa, and salt. Toss and stir with a fork. Add to the butter mixture and mix just until combined.

Turn out onto well-floured board and lightly roll with floured pin to $\frac{1}{4}$-inch-thick circle.

Cut into 2-inch circles (for "Faux Oreos" see page 72) or other shapes and transfer to ungreased cookie sheets. Bake just until set, 18 to 20 minutes. Transfer to racks to cool. Reroll remaining dough scraps, handling as lightly as possible, and repeat until no dough remains.

NOTE: Shortbread dough can be patted into individual tart pans, decorated with pecan halves, and baked a bit longer for a delightful mini–landing pad for vanilla ice cream.

MAKES 24

White chocolate is not really chocolate at all but a tablet of pressed sugar, cocoa butter, milk, and vanilla. Since it lacks cocoa liquor, it technically may not be labeled chocolate.

CHOCOLATE ALMOND BISCOTTI

For a dressier biscuit, dip half the biscotti in melted white chocolate or coat one side with "No-Fail Fudge Frosting" (see page 76).

1 stick butter, softened
2/3 cup sugar
2 eggs
1 teaspoon vanilla
1/2 teaspoon almond extract
1 1/2 cups all-purpose flour
1/3 cup ground almonds
1/3 cup Dutch cocoa
1 teaspoon baking powder
1/2 teaspoon salt
1/2 cup slivered almonds

Preheat oven to 350 degrees F.

Beat together butter and sugar until light and smooth. Add eggs, vanilla, and almond extract, and beat until smooth.

In another bowl, toss together flour, ground almonds, cocoa, baking powder, and salt. Add to the butter mixture and lightly beat until dough is formed. Gently stir in slivered almonds.

On lightly floured board, knead dough into ball and cut in half. Press each piece into a 10 x 4-inch loaf and transfer with a spatula to an uncoated baking sheet. Bake about 35 minutes, until set and dry. Cool on sheet 10 minutes and transfer to a board. Cut with a sharp knife into 1/2-inch slices across width. Return biscotti to sheet, cut-side up, and bake 10 minutes longer per side. Cool on racks and store.

MAKES 30

CHOCOLATE
COCONUT BARS

Here is a low-tech, hand-stirred brownie with a sweet coconut topping.

6 ounces semisweet chocolate, chopped
3 tablespoons butter
1/2 cup sugar
3 tablespoons water
2 eggs
3/4 cup all-purpose flour
1 1/4 cups flaked coconut
1/2 cup chopped pecans
1/3 cup semisweet chocolate chips
3/4 cup sweetened condensed milk

Preheat oven to 325 degrees F. Line an 8-inch square cake pan with parchment paper.

Combine chocolate, butter, sugar, and water in heavy saucepan. Cook over low heat, stirring constantly, until melted and smooth.

Transfer to mixing bowl. Whisk in
eggs and stir in flour until smooth.
Pour batter into pan, smoothing the top.
Bake 15 minutes.

Meanwhile, in another bowl, combine
coconut, pecans, and chocolate chips. Pour in
condensed milk and stir well. Spoon over partially baked chocolate, spreading in an even
layer out to edges. Return to oven and bake
until set, about 20 minutes. Cool in pan on
rack. Cut into small squares and transfer with
spatula to serving tray or tin.

MAKES 16 TO 20

CHOCOLATE CHERRY KISSES

These are dedicated to Helene's husband, a chocolate-covered-cherry addict.

1 stick butter, softened
1 cup sugar
2 eggs
1 teaspoon vanilla
$^1/_2$ teaspoon Kirsch
$1^3/_4$ cups all-purpose flour
$^1/_2$ cup Dutch cocoa
$^1/_2$ teaspoon baking soda
$^1/_2$ teaspoon salt
2 ($8^3/_4$-ounce) cans dark, sweet, pitted cherries in syrup, drained
4 ounces semisweet chocolate, chopped and melted

Preheat oven to 350 degrees F. Line
cookie sheets with parchment paper.

With electric mixer, cream together
butter and sugar until fluffy. Add eggs, vanilla, and Kirsch, and beat well.

In another bowl, combine flour, cocoa, baking soda, and salt. Add to butter mixture and
gently beat until flour disappears and dough is
smooth. Chill 20 minutes.

Drop dough by generous tablespoonfuls
onto prepared sheets, with 2-inch space
between. With a thumb, press a crater in the
center of each. Fill each with a drained cherry.
Bake about 15 minutes, just until set. Transfer
to racks to cool. Dip tines of a fork in melted
chocolate and drizzle over cooled cookies.
Place on plates and chill to set.

MAKES 24

TURTLE BROWNIES

Like the candies, these are tooth-achingly sweet and gooey.

2 ounces unsweetened chocolate, chopped
$\frac{1}{2}$ cup milk
1 stick butter
1 cup sugar
1 egg
1 cup all-purpose flour
$\frac{1}{4}$ teaspoon baking powder
1 teaspoon vanilla
$\frac{3}{4}$ cup chopped pecans
$\frac{1}{2}$ cup prepared caramel sauce

Preheat oven to 350 degrees F. Butter and flour an 8-inch square baking pan.

In small saucepan, combine chocolate and milk. Cook over medium-low heat, stirring frequently, until chocolate is melted. Set aside.

In medium bowl, cream together butter, sugar, and egg. Combine flour and baking powder and stir into butter mixture. Stir in chocolate mixture and vanilla. Fold in $1/3$ cup pecans. Transfer batter to prepared pan, smoothing the top. Bake 30 minutes. Set on rack to cool.

While brownies are still warm, spread caramel sauce over top, then sprinkle with remaining pecans. Cool completely and cut into 2-inch squares.

MAKES 16

DOUBLE MOCHA
BROWNIES

*Here's a fudgy, rich brownie laced with espresso
and Kahlua.*

4 ounces unsweetened chocolate, chopped
1½ sticks butter
2 tablespoons instant espresso powder
3 eggs
2 cups sugar
2 teaspoons Kahlua
1 cup all-purpose flour
¼ teaspoon salt
1 cup pecans, chopped

GLAZE
¼ cup plus 2 tablespoons confectioners' sugar
2 tablespoons Kahlua

Preheat oven to 350 degrees F. Line a 9 x 12-
inch pan with parchment.

Combine chocolate and butter in a heavy saucepan and melt over low heat, stirring until smooth. Stir in espresso to dissolve and set aside to cool.

In the bowl of an electric mixer, beat together eggs and sugar until smooth. Pour in cooled chocolate and beat to combine. Beat in Kahlua. Add flour and salt and beat until smooth and thick. Stir in pecans.

Spoon batter into prepared pan and bake about 35 minutes, until a tester comes out with moist crumbs clinging to it. Cool in pan on rack.

Make glaze by whisking together confectioners' sugar and Kahlua until smooth. Spread a thin layer over brownies, cut into squares, and remove from pan.

MAKES ABOUT 24

CHOCOLATE MERINGUE KISSES

$^1/_3$ cup Dutch cocoa
$^2/_3$ cup confectioners' sugar
4 egg whites, room temperature
$^1/_4$ teaspoon cream of tartar
$^1/_2$ cup sugar

Preheat oven to 225 degrees F. Line 2 baking sheets with foil. Lightly butter and flour foil. Fit large pastry bag with $^1/_2$-inch star tip.

Sift cocoa with confectioners' sugar into medium bowl.

In separate bowl, with electric mixer at medium speed, whisk egg whites with cream of tartar until soft peaks form. At high speed, gradually beat in granulated sugar, then continue to beat until meringue is shiny. Quickly but gently fold in cocoa mixture. Immediately spoon mixture into pastry bag. Pipe onto prepared baking sheets, making kisses about 2 inches in diameter at base and 1½ inches high and spacing them about 1 inch apart. Bake 1½ hours. Then turn oven off and dry kisses in oven at least 2 hours or until crisp and not sticky in center.

Kisses can be stored in airtight container up to 2 weeks. To recrisp, place in 200-degree oven 10 to 20 minutes, until dry.

MAKES ABOUT 36

Yes, chocolate is a fighting food; it supplies the greatest amount of nourishment in the smallest possible bulk.

         —Nestlé's World War II advertising slogan

DOUBLE CHOCOLATE
MACAROONS

$1/4$ cup Dutch cocoa
$1/4$ cup all-purpose flour
$1/2$ teaspoon baking powder
2 eggs
$3/4$ cup sugar
2 tablespoons butter, melted
$2^{1}/_{2}$ cups flaked coconut
1 cup semisweet chocolate chips

Preheat oven to 325 degrees F. Grease baking sheets.

Sift cocoa with flour and baking powder into medium bowl.

In separate bowl, beat eggs until foamy. Gradually beat in sugar, continuing to beat until thick and lemon colored. Blend in butter and stir in flour mixture. Fold in coconut. Drop by rounded teaspoonfuls, about 2 inches apart, on prepared sheets. Bake 15 minutes.

Transfer to racks to cool.

Line baking sheet with waxed paper.

Melt chocolate chips in the top of a double boiler or in the microwave. Holding each cookie by an edge, dip halfway into melted chocolate Set, right side up, on prepared baking sheet. Refrigerate to set. Store in single layer, covered, in refrigerator up to 5 days.

MAKES ABOUT 30

Chocolate as Health Food

The good news, according to the latest scientific findings, is that chocolate does not cause migraines, tooth decay, or skin eruptions. It is not habit forming, contains only minuscule traces of caffeine, and does not cause obesity. A one-ounce piece contains 150 calories. The bad news is that chocolate is poison for dogs. As little as two ounces of milk chocolate can make a ten-pound puppy wish he'd never seen the inside of a Hershey's wrapper.

TRIPLE CHIPPERS

2 cups all-purpose flour
1 teaspoon baking powder
1 teaspoon baking soda
$^1/_2$ teaspoon salt
1 cup shortening
1 cup brown sugar
1 cup sugar
2 eggs
1 teaspoon vanilla
2 cups rolled oats
$^3/_4$ cup each semisweet, milk, and white
  chocolate chips
$^1/_2$ cup chopped walnuts (optional)

Preheat oven to 350 degrees F. Grease baking sheets.

Stir together flour with baking powder, soda, and salt. Set aside.

In large bowl, cream shortening and sugars until light. Add eggs, one at a time, beating well after each addition. Stir in vanilla. Gradually stir in flour mixture until well blended. Stir in oats, chocolate chips, and walnuts. Drop by rounded tablespoonfuls, about 2 inches apart, on prepared baking sheets. Bake 12 to 15 minutes, or until edges are golden brown. Transfer to racks to cool.

MAKES ABOUT 6 DOZEN

It flutters you for a while, it warms you for an instant; then, all of a sudden, it kindles a mortal fever in you.
    —Madame de Sevigne

CHOCOLATE MOUSSE BARS

10 ounces milk chocolate, chopped
$\frac{1}{2}$ stick butter, melted
$1\frac{1}{4}$ cups crushed butter or shortbread cookies
$\frac{1}{2}$ cup finely chopped toasted almonds
1 cup heavy cream
8 ounces semisweet chocolate, melted and
    cooled slightly
2 tablespoons Dutch cocoa

Line 9-inch square pan with waxed paper, letting edges overhang sides.

In a medium saucepan, combine milk chocolate and butter. Place over medium-low heat and stir until chocolate is melted. Stir in cookie crumbs and almonds. Spread evenly over bottom of prepared pan. Chill to set.

In a clean bowl, whip cream until very thick. Fold in melted, cooled semisweet chocolate. Spread evenly over chilled layer. Chill at least 1 hour.

To serve, sift cocoa over top.
Remove from pan by pulling up on
waxed paper. Carefully cut into 1½ x 3-
inch bars and peel paper.

MAKES 18

Cortez's Discovery

*When it came to chocolate, Christopher Columbus
missed the boat. Though he brought it back with him to
Spain, it was considered bizarre and never caught on. It
took Cortez, who followed Columbus, to grasp the
importance of chocolate and to introduce it to skeptical
Europeans. By the time he landed in the Americas, the
Aztecs were using cacao beans as currency, and drinking
chocolate both hot and cold. Their leader, Montezuma,
thinking Cortez was the returning Quetzalcoatl, taught
him the finer points of chocolate processing and drinking—information that Cortez brought back with him to
Spain, where chocolate remained a well-kept secret and
a rich man's drink until word of it traveled to Italy sev-
enty years later.*

FAUX OREOS

If you have a favorite chocolate wafer recipe, you can substitute it for the shortbreads in this delightful sandwich cookie. The snow-white filling keeps in the refrigerator—let soften to spread.

1 recipe "Shortbreads from Heaven," (see page 52)

FILLING

⅓ cup vegetable shortening

1⅔ cups confectioners' sugar

2 tablespoons heavy cream

Bake the shortbreads and let cool.

Combine the shortening and sugar in the bowl of an electric mixer and beat well. Add the cream and continue beating at medium speed until smooth and spreadable, 2 to 3 minutes. Thinly spread filling on the bottom of one cookie, and cover with second cookie, bottom-to-bottom.

MAKES 12 SANDWICHES

LIFE-ENHANCING
FROSTINGS
&
TOPPINGS

MORE THAN CHOCOLATE GANACHE

This updated ganache can be used as a filling and frosting for layer cakes, as a mousse dessert, as a cream puff filling, or as a pie filling in a baked and cooled pastry or crumb crust.

2 cups heavy cream
5 ounces semisweet chocolate, chopped
1/2 teaspoon vanilla

In large bowl of electric mixer, combine 1 cup cream and the chocolate. Set over pan of simmering water until chocolate is melted, stirring to blend. Stir in remaining cream and vanilla. Chill at least 4 hours, stirring occasionally.
With electric mixer, beat on high speed until stiff.

MAKES ABOUT 4 1/2 CUPS, ENOUGH FOR TWO
10-INCH LAYER CAKES

NOTE: For classic ganache, use equal parts heavy cream and chocolate. Place chopped chocolate in a bowl and bring cream to a boil. Pour hot cream over chocolate, whisking until melted and smooth. Let sit at room temperature to thicken, and pour over cake.

Great Moments in American Chocolate

Though the first chocolate factory was started in 1765 by Dr. James Baker of Massachusetts, it wasn't until 1892 that America made great strides in chocolate. When candy manufacturer Milton Hershey of Pennsylvania attended the World's Fair in Chicago, he saw machinery that impressed him enough to sell his caramel factory and turn his full attention to chocolate—the wave of the future. Eventually he invented milk chocolate based on whole milk, substituted vegetable fats for cocoa butter for economy and stability, introduced almonds, and invented the six-ounce chocolate bar that became world famous as a war ration.

NO-FAIL FUDGE FROSTING

This frosting bears a striking resemblance to the thick, sweet, prepared kind sold in containers in the supermarket.

4 ounces unsweetened chocolate, chopped
2 tablespoons butter
3 cups confectioners' sugar
1/2 cup milk or half-and-half
1 teaspoon vanilla

Melt the chocolate and butter in a glass bowl in the microwave on high power, 1 minute, or in the top of a double boiler until smooth. Remove from heat.

To the chocolate mixture, add 1 cup of the sugar, milk or half-and-half, and vanilla. Whisk to combine. Gradually add remaining sugar, whisking until smooth and thickened to taste. Let sit about 10 minutes to thicken slightly.

MAKES 2 1/2 CUPS, ENOUGH FOR ONE 9-INCH TWO-LAYER CAKE

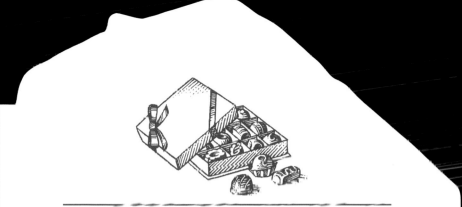

A World Tour of Chocolate

The Swiss, the world's largest per capita chocolate consumers, invented "conching," the process that smooths out chocolate and eliminates graininess. They also invented milk chocolate and are the proud producers of Lindt and Tobler.

A Dutchman, Coenraad Van Houten, invented the cocoa press, which made palatable chocolate widely available and eased the way for chocolate manufacture.

The world's largest chocolate factory is in America, in Hershey, Pennsylvania.

In England, where chocolate is virtually a dietary staple, it was popularized by Quaker-owned businesses such as Cadbury's and Rowntree's, whose owners viewed the chocolate business as preferable to gin. In Quaker Pennsylvania, Milton Hershey modeled Hersheyville after an English village.

SIMPLE
DARK CHOCOLATE GLAZE

We love a glaze like this on elegant one-layer cakes or brownies.

3 ounces semisweet chocolate, chopped
2 tablespoons sugar
1 tablespoon water
1 tablespoon liqueur such as Kirsch, rum, or Kahlua
2 tablespoons butter, softened

Combine chocolate, sugar, water, and liqueur in top of double boiler or in bowl over simmering water. Cook over low heat, stirring occasionally, until smooth and melted. Remove and stir in butter, a bit at a time, until smooth. Let sit at room temperature to thicken, about $1/2$ hour. Pour over cake, using a spatula to smooth.

MAKES $3/4$ CUP, ENOUGH FOR 1 CAKE

SOUR CREAM
CHOCOLATE FROSTING

*Here is an old recipe that will surprise you with
its ease and delicious flavor.*

5 ounces semisweet chocolate, chopped
pinch of salt
$\frac{1}{2}$ cup sour cream

Melt the chocolate in the top of a double boiler or in the microwave. Stir in salt and cool slightly. Add sour cream and stir until smooth.

MAKES $\frac{3}{4}$ CUP, ENOUGH FOR ONE CAKE

RENEE'S HOT FUDGE SAUCE

My favorite fudge sauce, from a terrific cook turned doctor, is dark and shiny, and clumps wonderfully when it hits cold ice cream.

5 tablespoons butter
4 ounces semisweet chocolate, chopped
$^1/_2$ cup sugar
$^2/_3$ cup heavy cream
pinch of salt
1 teaspoon vanilla

Combine butter, chocolate, sugar, and cream in heavy saucepan. Cook over low heat until butter and chocolate are melted. Whisk until smooth.

Turn heat to medium-high and bring to a boil, stirring occasionally. Remove from heat, stir in salt and vanilla, and pour over cold ice cream. Fudge sauce may be stored in the refrigerator up to 2 weeks. Reheat slowly, stirring frequently.

MAKES $1^1/_2$ CUPS

WHITE CHOCOLATE
SAUCE

*Serve with your favorite ice cream, as a dessert
sauce, or as a fondue for dipping fruits.*

$^2/_3$ cup heavy cream
2 cinnamon sticks, broken
6 ounces white chocolate, chopped
2 tablespoons almond liqueur such as Amaretto

In small saucepan, combine cream and cinnamon. Bring to full boil, remove from heat, cover, and let stand 15 minutes.

Meanwhile, place white chocolate in medium bowl. Return cream to boil, then pour through strainer into chocolate. Let stand 2 minutes, then stir until smooth. Stir in liqueur. Serve at room temperature or slightly warmed. Store in refrigerator.

MAKES $1^1/_4$ CUPS

SHAVED CHOCOLATE WHIPPED CREAM

This elegant whipped cream is white with chocolate dots.

2 ounces semisweet chocolate
1 cup heavy cream, cold
$1/4$ cup confectioners' sugar
$1/2$ teaspoon vanilla

Grate the chocolate against the small side of grater. Set aside.

Start whipping cream on medium-low speed of electric mixer. When it starts holding a shape, add sugar and vanilla. Turn speed to high and whip until soft peaks form. Gently fold in chocolate. Chill until serving time.

MAKES 2 CUPS

MAD MOUSSES,
PUDDINGS
&
TERRINES

BITTERSWEET MOUSSE

A suave, smooth pudding for classical French tastes.

5 ounces semisweet chocolate, chopped
2 tablespoons butter
4 eggs, separated
2 teaspoons rum, vanilla, or almond extract
pinch of salt
whipped cream or fresh berries for garnish

Combine the chocolate and butter in a heavy pan and melt over low heat, stirring frequently. Set aside to cool.

With an electric mixer, beat the egg yolks until smooth. Gradually pour the cooled chocolate mixture into yolks, beating until well combined. Beat in rum or extract.

In another bowl, whisk egg whites with salt until stiff peaks form. Gently fold into chocolate mixture until whites just disappear. Spoon into 6 small ramekins, cover with plastic wrap, and chill. Garnish to taste and serve cold.

SERVES 6

The Chocolate Tree

Theobroma cacao, *the original cocoa tree, a.k.a. "food of the gods," grew in the rain forests of the Amazon and Orinoco Rivers. It was first cultivated by the Mayans on the Yucatan peninsula to use in trade with the Aztecs of central Mexico. Like coffee, the cacao tree needs the rain and warmth that exists near the equator—twenty degrees north or south is best—and it needs the additional protection of "mother" trees, or shade trees, to protect it when it is young. Like coffee beans, cocoa beans depend on roasting to develop their intrinsic flavor. After roasting, the beans are crushed, milled, pressed, conched, combined, tempered, and molded to make bars of chocolate.*

CHOCOLATE ESPRESSO FLAN

A most delectable smooth and creamy flan.

1½ cups sugar
½ cup water
4 eggs
6 egg yolks
¾ cup brown sugar
3 cups half-and-half
2 tablespoons brewed espresso, cooled
2 tablespoons Kahlua
2 ounces semisweet chocolate, chopped
1 cup heavy cream

Preheat oven to 350 degrees F. Have ready a 10-inch round cake pan.

To make caramel, combine sugar and water in heavy medium saucepan. Cook over high heat until the sugar dissolves and liquid is clear. Reduce heat to medium-low and continue cooking until nut-brown and fragrant, 10

to 15 minutes. (Do not stir.)
Immediately pour into cake pan,
swirling to coat bottom and sides. Set
aside. (This can be done ahead.)

In large mixing bowl, gently whisk together
eggs, yolks, sugar, half-and-half, espresso, and
Kahlua.

Combine chocolate and 2 tablespoons of the
cream in heavy saucepan. Cook over low heat,
stirring frequently, until melted and smooth.
Add remaining cream, bring to a boil, and
remove from heat. Let cool. Pour cooled mixture
through strainer into egg mixture. Gently stir to
combine. Pour into caramel-lined pan.

Transfer to larger roasting pan and pour in
water halfway up sides of cake pan. Bake about 1
hour, until set. Remove from pan and let cool.
Cover with plastic and chill overnight.

To serve, run a knife around inside edge of pan to loosen and invert onto serving plate. (To loosen a reluctant flan, place on burner over low heat.) Spoon on any excess caramel and cut into wedges to serve.

SERVES 8

The Chocolate Legend in Mexico

According to Toltec legend, Quetzalcoatl, the plumed serpent, was sent by the gods to relieve the Toltecs' arduous lives. He bestowed upon them the cacao tree, previously exclusive to the gods, to lighten their load. But when they started roasting the beans, drinking xocolatl, *and trading the sacred beans as money, the gods felt betrayed and acted accordingly. They planted thorny mesquite trees in place of lush cacao, eventually causing the downfall of Quetzalcoatl and the Toltec civilization.*

MICHELLE'S
TWO-MINUTE MOUSSE

A foolproof recipe for instant chocolate pudding.

2 eggs
2 tablespoons rum or orange liqueur
2 teaspoons instant espresso powder
1 cup semisweet chocolate chips
3/4 cup hot milk
whipped cream for garnish

In blender, combine eggs, rum, espresso powder,
and chocolate chips. Pour in hot milk. Cover
and process on high 1 to 2 minutes or until
smooth. Pour mixture into 4 small bowls or
stemmed dessert dishes. Chill at least 1 hour.
Serve with dollops of whipped cream.

SERVES 4

GINGER POTS DE CREME

These sensuous puddings hold a crisp surprise on the bottom—tart bits of crystallized ginger.

$1/4$ cup finely diced crystallized ginger
3 egg yolks
1 egg
1 cup half-and-half
4 ounces semisweet chocolate, chopped

Preheat oven to 325 degrees F. Divide the ginger and place in the bottom of 6 oven-proof
$1/2$-cup ramekins or custard cups. Arrange the cups in a larger roasting pan and pour in water halfway up the sides of cups.

In a medium bowl, gently whisk together egg yolks and whole egg.

Pour half-and-half into small saucepan and bring nearly to a boil. Add chocolate, stir, and remove from heat. Continue stirring until smooth and melted. Let cool. Pour cooled chocolate into eggs and mix with a spoon just to combine. Ladle into prepared cups and cover loosely with foil.

Bake about 40 minutes, until sides are set and center loose. Remove cups from pan, cover, and transfer to refrigerator. Chill at least 2 hours.

SERVES 6

HOT COCOA SOUFFLÉ

butter for coating
$1/2$ cup plus 2 tablespoons sugar
$1/3$ cup Dutch cocoa
$1/4$ cup all-purpose flour
pinch of salt
1 cup half-and-half
$1/2$ teaspoon vanilla
4 eggs, separated
whipped cream for garnish

Preheat oven to 350 degrees F. Generously butter a $1^1/2$-quart soufflé dish and sprinkle with 2 tablespoons sugar.

In medium saucepan, combine $1/4$ cup of the sugar with the cocoa, flour, and salt. Gradually stir in half-and-half. Cook over medium heat, stirring constantly, until mixture boils and thickens. Remove from heat and stir in vanilla.

In large bowl of electric mixer,
whisk egg whites until foamy.
Gradually add remaining ¼ cup sugar.
Continue whisking at high speed until stiff
and glossy.

In small bowl, lightly beat egg yolks. Stir
into reserved chocolate mixture. Gently fold
chocolate mixture into egg whites. Carefully
transfer to prepared dish and bake 30 to 40
minutes, until puffy but wobbly in the center.
Serve immediately with whipped cream.

SERVES 6

---

*I love chocolate. I love the way it comes wrapped in
thin silvery foil and heavy-grade paper, and the way
it is molded into little squares and the way it feels in
my mouth.*

> —*Loru Brody, author of* Growing Up on the
> Chocolate Diet

BITTERSWEET
SORBET

*This intense, sweet shot of pure chocolate would
make a nice ending for an elegant summer meal.*

6 ounces bittersweet chocolate, chopped
$^1/_2$ cup sugar
$1^1/_2$ cups water

Melt the chocolate in the top of a double boiler
or in the microwave. Set aside to cool.

Combine sugar and water in small saucepan.
Cook over high heat, stirring occasionally, until
a clear syrup forms. Let cool.

When both mixtures are cool, pour both into
mixing bowl and stir well. Chill an hour or two.
Pour into ice cream maker and process according
to manufacturer's instructions. Transfer to covered plastic container and freeze until serving
time. Let soften slightly to serve.

MAKES 2 CUPS, SERVES 4

CONVERSIONS

LIQUID
  1 Tbsp = 15 ml
  $\frac{1}{2}$ cup = 4 fl oz = 125 ml
  1 cup = 8 fl oz = 250 ml

DRY
  1/4 cup = 4 Tbsp = 2 oz = 60 g
  1 cup = $\frac{1}{2}$ pound = 8 oz = 250 g

FLOUR
  $\frac{1}{2}$ cup = 60 g
  1 cup = 4 oz = 125 g

TEMPERATURE
  400° F = 200° C = gas mark 6
  375° F = 190° C = gas mark 5
  350° F = 175° C = gas mark 4

MISCELLANEOUS
  2 Tbsp butter = 1 oz = 30 g
  1 inch = 2.5 cm
  all-purpose flour = plain flour
  baking soda = bicarbonate of soda
  brown sugar = demerara sugar
  confectioners' sugar = icing sugar
  heavy cream = double cream
  molasses = black treacle
  raisins = sultanas
  rolled oats = oat flakes
  semisweet chocolate = plain chocolate
  sugar = caster sugar